Garden Physic

Also by Sylvia Legris

The Hideous Hidden

Pneumatic Antiphonal

Nerve Squall

Iridium Seeds

Circuitry of Veins

GARDEN PHYSIC

Sylvia Legris

with maps, illustrations, and photographs by the author

A New Directions Paperbook Original

Manufactured in the United States of America
First published as a New Directions Paperbook (NDP1516) in 2021
Design by Marian Bantjes

Library of Congress Cataloging-in-Publication Data
Names: Legris, Sylvia, author, illustrator.
Title: Garden physic / Sylvia Legris ; with maps and illustrations by the author.
Description: New York, NY : New Directions Publishing Corporation, 2021.
Identifiers: LCCN 2021031344 | ISBN 9780811229906 (paperback) |
ISBN 9780811229913 (ebook)
Subjects: LCGFT: Poetry.
Classification: LCC PR9199.3.L3945 G37 | DDC 811/.54—dc23
LC record available at https://lccn.loc.gov/2021031344

10 9 8 7 6 5 4 3 2 1

New Directions Books are published for James Laughlin
by New Directions Publishing Corporation
80 Eighth Avenue, New York 10011

ndbooks.com

and gardens exist, horticulture, the elder tree's
pale flowers, still as a seething hymn

— Inger Christensen
(*translated by Susanna Nied*)

Contents

The Yard Wants What the Yard Wants

caragana

Plants Reduced to the Idea of Plants

The flourish, the fanfare, the febrifugic feverfew.

An oleaginous emplastrum—with horehound leaf,
olive over olive, the oily parts, the dry.

An antidote for the unblessed, the blistering,
the dourly flowering flora, the corpse flora.

Greek turned Latin turned inordinately
angled and filed.

Plants reduced to the idea of plants reduced to woodcuts
(circa 16th century) reduced to Victorian floor tile.

Travel by river snail, by liver of mad dog.
By God Greek Juniper! By monoxide of lead.

Travel under government of the moon
with arrach wild and stinking.

Flower and seed through August from June.
The butcher, the barber, the oil-boiling cauterizer.

The vegetal assiduousness, the pennywort diligence.

Plants Further Reduced to the Idea of Plants

1st: Confirm
the morphological integrity of the garden body.
Ignore the blood and hairy root saw,
the skin under its nails garden claw.
Expose the corpus hortus siccus,
the corpus exsiccatae.

2nd: Field
the spiral-rung, the stitched, the strung,
the Cerlox-spined, the glue-gunned,
the Duo-Tanged (*le cerveau bilingue*),
the never perfect perfect-bind,
the Peterson-worthy field guide.

3rd: Forget
the church fathers, the philosophers,
the appropriate and inappropriate authorities.
Forget the know-it-all anthologists,
the squirrelers of curios and collectibles.

The Garden Body: A Florilegium

1

A pepper of bees opens the pupils.   *An ensemble of aromatics*
Chorus aphrodisia, mariner's root,
bright sky and night star, heavenly
rainbow. Amethyst, azure, blue
flower de luce. Flowering ring.

...

White archangelic the bee nettle,
the dead nettle. A hide of nettle cloth,
of finely nerved sedge. Take heed
the edges, the pipes, the passages,
the petal corridor, the corolla tube.

...

A blossom is a throat. Rose-oil and hip.
A ripped rose is a voice organ, time-cut
and curt. Royally red and confidence-
keeping, redder than Mars, redder than
hot days and parched, Venus on the lips.

2

Muscle rose. Flesh rose.
Then rustling redshank rose.
Vines ascend the arch of aorta.
Mercurial, the climbing nightshade,
the bundle-branched bittersweet.

A verge toward red

...

White-spotted hellebore under Jupiter
and wind. Oak lungs, jovial lungs.
Sea rush blows the lungs with sweet rose,
carmine and sanguine, flaming red.
Candleberry fires the blood.

...

Red is antispasmodic, cardiovascular.
Great garden patience of Mars.
May-blossom, hawthorn. Spring
gushes red-veined with sorrel, bloodwort
below Jupiter, red dock for longevity.

3

Venus stokes the throatwort.   *Ringing with wasps*
The good leaf. The rose noble.
L'herbe du siège slackens
the isthmus of the fauces.
Gash-red and choking rose.

...

Double tongue. Bay laurel.
Daphne of the sun.
Yarrow charms wasps,
snuffs the inveterate headache.
Daphne sings the bees from the ears.

...

The voice reeds are a Queen Anne's lace
of wasps. Mercury abounds with buzz
and wild carrot, jumpstarts speech
with hoar-strange words, a gargle
of hog's fennel and brimstonewort.

4

Under Leo, composure.   *Touchwood and rue*
Herb of grace. Anti-magical.
Vinegar of the four thieves.
Poison against poison. Rue before regret.
Touch wood ruta sets the garden free.

...

Lightning sulfur the garden prone
to primrose and paroxysm. Pellitory-
of-the-wall quells old hacking. An old cough.
A new moon courtesy of wild clary.
Eyebright. Clear eye (*en toute bonne foi*).

...

Sweep away the broom, the burdock,
the beastly antipathy between ash tree
and adder. Snakeweed. Dragon's blood.
Devil's bit. Serpent's tongue. Wickedness
(a weak moon) licked & licked & licked.

5

What a commotion! Wild rocket, a racket   *Flesh and blood*
of wake robin, cuckoo point, the clear
caroling rise & fall. Volatile dog's mercury.
Dog's-grass. Dog rose. Hot fits and cold
metallic blue. The indecisive indigo.

...

So the garden bellyaches. So what
the gripes? Rows rife with tormentil,
gallant herb of the sun. Five fingers,
flesh and blood. Stamina, life's long
thread, root-red, the unhindered heart.

...

Leaves respire and rain returns blood-veined
and blood dock, blood-colored juices. Red poppy
a headache. Heartichoke the downhearted.
Loosestrife calms the fugitive scarlet.
Sweet slumber. The fleshy rootstock.

6

Enlist imagination under the banner of science.   *Erasmus Darwin,*
Flora attired by the elements.   *his Botanic Muse*
Sea lavender, sea holly, sundrops.
Jacob's ladder reaching ether.
Wind rose. Sun rose. Water grass.

...

The loves of the plants. (The economy of vegetation.)
Root, pith, lobes, plume, calyx, coral, sap.
Air distributes the seeds of names.
Windflower, digitalis. Tipsy and ethereal.
Trade winds, vital light. Seeds within seeds.

...

Start from the soil, and win their airy way.
The fifty-seeded heart's delight, saturnine
and doting wild. Heart's-ease. Herb constancy.
Pensée ... An opening. Call-me-to-you. Kiss-her-
in-the-buttery. Meet-me-in-the-entry.

7

The yard wants what the yard wants.   *Rose*
Bloom of Ruth. Breath of life. Blush.
Charisma. Compassion. Imagination.
Ebb tide and nostalgia. Groundcover
and climbers. Floribunda. Abundance.

...

A hybrid of bruise and steep, petal and dreg.
Lungfuls of lamp flower, rose campion,
rose of heaven. The moon shoulders roseroot,
rosy-colored stonecrop. The neck laced with
French rose, common rose, pomander of roses.

...

At the center of the garden the heart.
Red as any rose. Pulsing
balloon vine. Love in a puff.
Heartseed, heart-of-the-earth.
A continuous flow of red.

8

Nosebleed, staunchweed, sanguinary.   *List*
Thousand-leaved root of yellow.
Thousand weed with leaves like feathers.
Small birds flirt herb-of-Venus' tree.
If my love love me, nosebleed and yarrow.

...

Feverfew-profuse June and July.
Agueweed, sweating-plant,
boneset with yellow thrum.
Venus yields to water.
Boneset breaks the sun.

...

Past mudwalls and molehills,
where the cowslips and the lungs moss,
hedge bells, morning glory and the hundred-leaved
rose, all the livelong organs rose—
a catalogue, a desire, a wish.

9

Chaffweed whups the chin-cough.   *Life everlasting*
Venus hiccups dry wind and sandy rows.
The garden ruminates cudweed,
creeping roots June through September.
Pearl-flowered. Eternal flower.

...

Take flower-gentle.
Take knitbone and knitback.
Ass ear. Blackwort. Slippery root.
Saturn's orbit comfrey-picked and sea-goat-prickly.
Take sea wrack, knobbed wrack, bladderwrack.

...

Forget-me-not. Forget-me-not. Forget-me-not.
Mouse-ear to the ground. Borage for courage.
Self-heal. All-heal. By crook or by hook-heal.
Paralysis and palsywort the garden
supplants fool's parsley with imperatives!

10

La voilà! Horsetail and paddock-pipes.   *Viola organista*
A hurdy-gurdyish drone.
Pansy-meek with cattail and fretted tension.
(Love-in-idleness.)
The over-thinking viola.

...

Liverwort, liverleaf, liverweed. A low sun
and Jupiter presumes three-lobed hepatica.
Water hectors wind and wind blows sound
into lungwort, bladderwort, kidneywort,
the kidney-leaved sower weed, the hartwort.

...

Dame de coeur. The crowning heart.
The garden wants it all: leaf, stem, root,
the whole shooting match shoot system,
timbre, pitch, fully chromatic rows,
heart trefoil and arssmart under sun.

Where Horsetail Intersects String

quillwort

Equisetum hyemale (Rough Horsetail)

after a photograph by Karl Blossfeldt

Let the fossil record show:

Green of two winters;
Small scale fluctuations;
Multi-tempoed scouring-rush;

Rough scrub-music horsetail;
Amplified 40-fold brusque bray;
Silica-encrusted corrugations;

A living fossil cross-section;
Reedy wetland habitat;
Pewterwort the sonorous tin-herb;

Cone an E-flat apiculate pitch.

Ferns and Fern Allies

The great fern radiation.
The origin of the dysfunctional family: spores.
Friend or foe? True fern or ally?
Extend a hand the fingers curl like a violin scroll.
The chin rests on a wet scouring rush.
Flat vascular depression upsets the pitch range.
Acoustics thick-walled and globose.
A music of neither seed nor flower.
Terrestrial chimeric. An amalgam.

Bladder-fern. Adder's-tongue.
Where horsetail intersects string.
Where tone color is quillwort.
Spiny-spored or large-spored?
Bristle tips or conspicuous tufts?
Upper bout an upswept moonwort.
Lower bout a smooth woodsia.
Diminutive growing in low fronds.
Rhizomes erect to ascending in perfect fifths.

Catkin-Bearing Trees and Shrubs

Pollination by wind and a long-held note.
Spring's purr neither feline nor familial.

The woody scale of a fruiting catkin.
Flared like the bell of a B-flat clarinet.

Head-to-head air currents. An auditory swing.
A tête-à-tête of anthers and stigmas.

A semitone lower? Floral bracts before leaves.
The precocious-flowering pussy willow.

Palette of open alluvial woods, seepage slopes.
Hoary willow notes of marly bog and fen.

Sweet gale and myrtle. *Myrica*'s waxy catkins.
Fragrance a wave that propagates air.

Timbre? Deciduous or evergreen.
Drupe-like fruits. Wing-like bracteoles.

Or the red-brown bark of false mountain willow.
Longitudinal splits. Yellowish overtones.

Violet

A garland to fend off the dizzies.
A garland to keep the quinsy at bay.
March closes the seeded umbilicus.
April opens the musty secundina.
Equinox the half-melt rot.
Easter the thin asquintable light.

Viola

Under Venus the sugared wound, the heart-strung-up, the viola d'amore.
Under Venus the Pliny-prescribed, the horsehair hanked—not plucked,
tugged—the singly sung (catgut kidney-cuffs the caterwaul, a knockback
to the viola bastarda). Kittenish! A scalloped flirtatious border—florid
cordial pansies (candied adoration). *Viola odorata*. Parfait d'Amourish.

White Flower II

after a painting by Agnes Martin

Canvas

Springbeauty. The eye unblanks the mesa. Solitary & leafless.
White tackstem. Common yarrow. Wild plum. A disciplined
plumb line. Boundless butte: a perfect geometry. Midvein math
of spreading sandwort (100 yellow disc florets). Fibonacci the
daisy tidytips. The radially symmetrical rose heath, ray-bright.

Heather the bell-ringer. Mountain pea, pony beebalm, phlox.
Fringepod & pricklyleaf, the dense rosettes of Buckley's yucca.
Four-o-clock verbena the high tableland wavers. Repeating
alkali marsh aster. Saltwort. Saxifrage. Mudbrick and grid.
Adobe. Abide, in unblinking light. Blazing star. Sacred datura.

Taos

Sweet Alison. O sweetclover. Chickweed. Chicory. Alyssum.
Alpine pennycress, Rocky mountain pussytoes, watercress and
bittercress (heartleaf). Tufted evening primrose, cutleaf & pale
primrose, gravel ghost, angel's trumpet, shade-loving angelica.
Desert rosemallow, marsh marigold, smallflower sand verbena.

Springbeauty (lanceleaf, scattered). Blooms for blooms' sake:
star lily, woolly bluestar, fringed grass of Parnassus. Raspberry
(New Mexico). Popcorn flower (Arizona). Plateau pepperwort.
Pepperweed and carelessweed. Doubting mariposa lily. Cream
cinquefoil. White violet. Desert zinnia. Two-toned everlasting.

Macklin

Blue-eyed Mary. The tall meadow rue, the veiny meadow rue,
the northern blue-eyed grass. Eyebright and downy paintbrush.
Wild white geranium, wild wild strawberry. Whorled milkweed
moreover, white flowers in terminal umbels. Sandwort, the dry
dry soil. White-prairie clover, white-flowered parsley, gentian.

Springbeauty (the linear-leaved). The many-flowered aster, the
rayless aster, willow aster and rush (leaves level, sessile, stem-
clasping and steadfast). Bindweed, buck-bean, bellflower. Then
cow parsnip, ox-eye daisy. Cow-wheat & milkwort. And lastly,
anemone (heartache-flower): long-fruited; wood anemone; tall.

Root of Scarcity

To sow the remote morose root.
To sow the virtuous standby.
The backup fodder-crop suffers not
from seasonal vicissitudes,
mildew and blast, caterpillar attack.

Under Saturn sing the golden-sickled beet.
Under Saturn sing the ringed mangelwurzel.
The great turnip (the dick reuben!).
The pickled paucity-strick stew.

Corn Crowfoot, Corn Buttercup

Ranunculus, little frog, *grenouillette*,
Mars blisters above neap flood and neck,
mustard-nasal, the rheum and runny river,
adenoidal, tongue-sore, the decoct & decant,
the goats, the pigs, also cows turn their backs,
worms compelled to flee the earth—the toxic
hop, the spirit-inflammation, the fiery.

Grasscloth

Two-weight brocatelle. Historic plaited gold.
A wide-looming lea. A no seamed sea.
Raised, ribbed, leaf-sheathed and spikeletted.
Handloomed broad-glumed brome.
Yards and yards of yellow and yellow.

Grasscloth (Millefleur)

Flatlands of irregularity.
Scroll. Littlescroll.
Trail-patterning *Flora.*

*

So wields the needle-
and-threaded grass, the dyer's weld,
the thousand-flowered dye book. Wild bluebell,
bellwort, bugleweed, the ecclesiastical ding-

dong, the chime, the chintz of *Sistine* and *Trinitas,*
woven silk and cotton, poppy linen.

Under the block-printed willow bough.
Where hawthorn and hyssop collide.
A back-lit haute-lisse crashes the colorway.

Wallpaper

The walls a garland of woe. *Poppy* and *Wreath*. A wind-around of lineage and plant. Velvet and vine. Larkspur on saddened madder. Chestnut cocktail, iron acetate. Autumn rose. A ghost of acanthus.

William Morris in His Disappointment Garden

Damp-squib grammar of pretty things and wild mignonette.
Quercitron bark. Old fustic's persistently pissy stamen,
the peony-stained wallpaper. Despite the conspicuous hot spots,
sun, chrysanthemum, coreopsis, yellow's a letdown nevertheless.

The repeating motifs? Killers. Jasmine twill, jasmine trellis ...
Trifoliate moth-traps these wool and cotton undersellers.
Envisage *Little Chintz* or *Corncockle* (where the flower plays
but a minor part), or an indigo-discharged rose. And the bugs!

Kermes, cochineal. A scuffle of ripe and ruin among rosebud
and campion, columbine and vine. So heartsunk am I of tusser silk
and cotton velveteen. Fuffling if nothing this art of color or perish.
Lacking compassion for lac-dye and up to the elbows in vermillion

melodrama ... *I'm dyeing, I'm dyeing ...*

Floral Correspondences

Nature must prick us with her courages also.
— Vita Sackville-West

Frost and snow. Our poor garden.
— Harold Nicolson

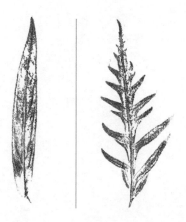

milkweed/fern-leaf golden elderberry

My Darling,

A disagreement of winter and spring and I refuse to be disconsolate. Light incurs ice. *Suns sink on suns.* My jottings of flowers crush the last chilly flourishes (plots and plots of ideas!). I am flush with anticipation. (You in all my notes to self.)

—V.

Dear,

I imagine everything in full fig.
Dug up and dragged.
The stone coping.
The windows' weepy wails.

Under your gumboots a grumbling of over-the-top bulbs.
Pale noses yet to surface.
Slug bait at the ready.
The ground rumbling.

—H.

My Dear Love,

Mad March dreams
of crane flowers,
birds of paradise.
Strelitzia reginae a deft cut
of bird and flower.

Sunbirds perch and powder
their breasts with pollen—
pollinators who sail the seasons.
(A rare plant who prefers birds over insects
am I.)

—V.

My Dear,

Haphazard jottings.
A lawn of daffodils.
A waterlogged orchard.
A union of heat and damp.

A lone osmanthus, white-clustered, apricot-smelling.
Balsam poplar takes me by the nose.

What endures?
Viburnum in full flower.
Recklessly planted corners.
My faith in deadheading.

—V.

My Darling,

The threat of frost supplanted by a dummy run of white and grey.

I'm scheming lavender, clematis, primrose. A corner of lilies and
camellias. A low feast of grey foliage. Artemisia and cotton lavender.
A high yew hedge. Grey and white edging: Rabbits' Ears, Savior's Flannel.

An experiment of apparition and whim.
A good great ghost of a garden!

—V.

My Dear Love,

How to write about flowers without the nauseating sentimental phraseology? No quaint, no dainty, no winsome. This smells good, that smells bad, my hands rank with manure. This at least is pure.

—V.

Oh Darling,

Midges and tetchiness.
A constantly muddy mood.

In my impatience for mail it strikes me that the perianth is a floral
envelope—a cloak concealing the reproductive organs ...

Alas, I forbear. A capacity for waiting defines both the gardener and the
letter-writer (the growing season longer than my endurance). I throw
myself into work and diversion but progress so slowly I fear there will be
frost by the time this reaches you. Snow on your salpiglossis.

—H.

O' My Love,

Busy Lizzie. Wink and blink. Touch-me-not. Impatiens as ever a virtue my dear! Enough of this love your perennials and they will love you back threefold and several seasons. If you don't like it, pull it out! My sweetbriars are scraggy at the roots and anemically unremarkable—my backstairs darlings. I have enfeebled them with too much devotion.

—V.

My My My,

The wide sweep of today.
Books, flowers, and poetry. Woolgathering and trees.
The wood garden is fervor, a blaze of primula and anemone.
The poplar is passion, viola-resonant, my vibrating footfall.

Not a weed in sight, lupines and irises, perfect turf.
The Hugh Dickson under the bedroom window
—my classic hybrid tea, my repeat rose—
buds patience and patience.

—V.

My Own Own Darling,

Pegging perpetual roses.
Bourbon roses.
Hybrid perpetuals.
Cut-and-come-again.
Cut-and-come-again.
Rose shoots
tied at intervals.
Rose shoots
twined in a half-hoop.
The wall plants,
the post-and-wired.

My dear,
ask only for a generous *floraison*:
the deliberate flowers,
the thoughtful,
the single-bloomed,
the fully double.
You can't ask everything of a plant.

—V.

My Dear Love,

Each day the light diminishes earlier. Colors at dusk are softer with an opulence they lack under full sun. My eyes strain with the beautiful painful squint. My wax flowers, my painter's palette—a floral encaustic! The papery papavers are waxy in the frigid morning air, but by noon I can see my fingers through them, fluttering, a swim of color, red under red.

"The poppy in her radiance is translucent," wrote Lawrence. Not the unalloyed red of the Adonis-blood anemone, but Vonnoh's fiery cadmium, blood with a drop of sulfide. What was his painting? ... *Les coquelicots—Entre une plaquemine et une orange sanguine.* Somewhere between persimmon and blood orange. *Une goutte de couleur.*

My heart flowers, drop by drop ...
Out the window my love lies bleeding.

—V.

Dearest,

Some thoughts on shade.

I screen my eyes against sun a shade of canary bird zinnia.
Yellow is remembrance, the scent of an absent friend.
Red is steadfastness, the heart, a hummingbird chasing nectar.

On the north side of the house rhododendrons,
the shade-loving azaleas, a splendid contradiction
of charming and lethal—mad honey—
the thinking-of-home-bush, the affections held back.

—H.

Darling,

Je fais ce que je peux.
Which is to say midwinter
and poems are as difficult as flowers.
Roots are secrets, my heart
mulch-heavy—a flowering shrub
under leaves and leaves,
rotting beech and oak.
I do what I can which is to say
there is little going on above ground.

—V.

DE MATERIA MEDICA

(after Pedanius Dioscorides)

rhubarb bolted

BEING AN HERBAL
WITH MATERIALS MEDICINAL AND BUCOLIC
WITH RHYMES AND COLIC

WRITTEN IN ENGLISH IN THE TWENTY-FIRST CENTURY OF THIS UNCOMMON ERA

THE CONTENTS

THE OATH

NOT THROUGH VANITY NOR IMPULSIVENESS
WITH MINIMAL OMISSIONS

IGNORE NOT USEFUL ROOTS
RESIST MEAGER DESCRIPTIONS

BEAR UP—DETRACTORS
ANOINT THEIR CLAWS WITH WORDS

FORECAST THE VERBS
WEATHER THE ADJECTIVES

THE DEDICATION

LO DEAREST AREIUS

FORGIVE THE POETS FOR BEING SYSTEMICALLY UNSYSTEMATIC
THE CONFLATION OF CHAOS AND COMMONPLACE

UNHEED THE ERRONEOUS NEEDLING
UNFEED THE NEEDLESS CONTROVERSIES

OIL THE LIPS WITH OINTMENTS AND UNGUENTS
RESIN THE INTENTIONS WITH GUMS OF TREES

TAKE THESE RECIPES WITH PRUDENCE AND ACID
VOLATILE SALTS   ANTHELMINTICS   EMOLLIENTS

SO BLOOMS

bluebell

In which is assembled the many plants for whom I have tender affection.
Fertilized and abridged. Rendered and weeded.
Of the storing the gathering the proper harvest.
In which I attempt to elucidate varieties and uses.
Methods of preparation.
Ordeals and tests.
The potent and the useless.

Prelude

The history of botany is the history of pharmacy.
Plants for easing pain, plants for easing sleep.
Plants to ward off windy afflictions and poisonous beasts.
Plants for weakness of the stomach and eyes that weep.
Plants that scream when pulled from the ground.
Plants that purify the earth.
Plants aseptic and plants for the skeptic.
Plants of antiquity and plants impending.
Plants that balm the living and plants that preserve the dead.

Earth that yields violet to brass.
Earth that smacks of ash.
Alkaline earth, bastard earth.
Earth that appeases the body and eases the mind.

Flowers of Brass [Book 5.88]

Part 1. Indissoluble Earth

This first poem about the last book is where the garden begins.
Sand and prolific dust.
Metals and earth.
Earth like small coals from a pitch tree.
Burnt red earth.
Big-veined bituminous earth.

*

Supreme earth has the disposition of medicine.
Earth that cools the pores.
Earth that closes cuts and heals sores.

Earths capable of absorbing acids.
Earths aluminous with spores.
The forgotten earths, the excavated.
The earths of bones and horns.

*

Animals and earth.
Vegetables and earth.
Geodes, whetstone, soot, and earth.

*

Pharmacy begins in plants.
Plants are the flesh of the Gods.
In the Kingdoms of Nature the final authority is earth.

Part 2. Flowers of Brass

The virtues of earth are the virtues
of guts, gall, metallurgy, and nerve.

Earths showy and not showy.
Earths sapid and insipid.
Earth that tastes of copper and zinc.
Earth as bland as coral and chalk.

*

So sits the garden in vegetable pride.
Plotted in graphite and plumbago.
Strange metals and stranger flowers.
Gold salts and leadwort, frothy silver.

A garden of Cyprian earth fired in kilns.
A garden of white lead scraped and pounded.
Flowers of cadmium from red-hot brass.
Of brass burnt from the nails of ships.

*

Silver slag, iron slag, lead slag.
Petals and leaves spit from earth.
Seeds of metallic scales.
Scales like glittering millet.
Brass in the pitch of thundering Zeus.
Brass in the scale of a Delphic hymn.

Part 3. Chaff

Flowers inscribed on stone.
Flowers in a single melodic line.
Alloy shavings.
The brassy chaff.
Flowers of chutzpah and cheek.

*

The yard is a measure of several millennia.

A yard of stars and amalgams.
A yard of grama grass and asters.
Day's eyes and damned yellow composites.
Petals that open at dawn and close at dusk.

Flowers with conspicuous bracts.
Grasses circled by hair.
Spikelets housing tiny flowers.
Florets of malleable elements.

*

Needlegrass.
Saltgrass.
Alkaligrass.
A choir of melicgrass.
Wry wry the wild rye!

[Book 2]
Lyme grass, marram grass, matgrass.
Darnel and cheat. A suppository of emmer wheat.

Habitat

Bentgrass interrupted.
Redtop and creeping bent.
Lake margins and drying shores.
Vernally flooded streams.

Disturbed ground including shores of moving water.
Disturbed areas adjacent to freshly seeded lawn.
Gardens and other human-disturbed places.
Waste places and roads, roadsides and ditches.

Spare the ferule and proliferate the fescue.
Clearings and sand dune complexes.
Rocky banks and eroded prairie hillsides.
An infinity of motes of minor value, twigs and straws.

Bluff, bluff, bluff, then fells of foothills fescue.
Slopes of bluebunch and proliferous red.
Brush meadow highs and anklebone lows.
Scree fields and debris, talus slopes.

River-rush, prairie-rush, spike-rush and club-.
Hairy and knotted, the confusing rush.
The many-flowered rush of muskeg and peaty shore.
Ravine slopes, ravine bottoms, sloughs.

[Book 4]
Poet's jasmine to oil the senses.
Poet's narcissus to loosen the joints.
Poet's cassia to tap the roots.

Origins of the Poem

1. Sepia [Book 2.23]
Byproducts of chemical deterrence.
Taste-by-touch startle displays.
Phagomimicries.
Atrocious pen-and-ink fish.
Ink-slinking cuttlefish.

Pseudomorph decoys.
Ink amended with mucous.
Shells rubbed on rough cheeks.
Crusty matter pounded to powder and pill.
Cuttlebones of buoyancy.

2. Ink [Book 5.183]
Paintings executed by fire or heat.
Documents signed with shellfish and soot.
Soot gathered from torches.
Soot mingled with Benjamin gum.
Antiseptic pastes of bulls' glue and soot.

Glass-making spinoffs.
Tree tumors and gall.
Burned copper and blue vitriol.
Neolithic lamb's-tongue tattoos.
Thick salves that grow new skin.

*

Plants for rough tongues and running ears,
for honeycombed ulcers and dreams of bees.

Plants as antidotes, as amulets,
for broken bones and broken flesh.

Plants for dull sight,
for falls from heights.

Plants for flatulence, for fear of water,
for nostrils flowing with blood.

So Blooms—

the remedial florilegia.
By the dog the minced oaths,
the god-wounds, the solemnly
declared chronical maladies.
The bloody blankety blank ...

So blooms
some small vulgarity.
The bad-rhyming carrion.
These unpoetical Asclepiads.
(Unmetrically unsucculent.)

The open wound-stenched.
The rot-ponged.
The rodenty.

Plants that draw out bile and phlegm,
that draw out broadworms and blood.

Plants to expel:
fish, fleas, flies and foxes, leeches, lice and nits.

Plants for bites of rodents and bites of vipers,
bites of mad dogs and bites of men.

Waste-eliminating plants and sin-purging plants.
Plants as enchantments and love-medicine plants.

So Blooms—

a vial of *viola tricolor.*

Orchard-bruised and unimpeachable.
Lungs clingy, windblown, heavy-huffed
with wild pansy, prussic, muzzily trussed.

Swig the cordial, the unpeachy lovelorn,
the falling-in falling-down sickness potion.
Lolly the asthmatic, the untamed wheezy.

Saturnine with hawkweed and horsetail.
Wild-thoughted summer and spring.
Cull me. Cuddle me. Call-me-to-you.
Pink-o'-the-Eye. Banewort. Constancy.

By the hair of the rampion.
Bell-flowered and ringing love.
Morning glory loves in vain.
Marigold despairs.

Mourn the vernal equinox.
Pour asphodel in purulent ears.
Cook the roots in ashes.
Regret follows to the grave.

'Struth—

the killing dead weight.

'Struth the cruelty in the extreme.
The great pains not taken—God's truth
love-in-idleness cross the heartsease!
The three-colored, the three-faced inflamed.

[Book 1]
Oils, ointments, and trees.
The liquors, the gums, and the fruits that come of them.

"Pick me ..."

Peals the self-serving physic garden.
Gold-leafed in leaps and zounds
burgeons the marginalia,
the gleaming illuminations.

Premorbid and full-of-promise
these plant-stranded pages. O cruets
of ignorance. O cruets of bless
this body being pleasingly invested.

The balmy-sweet, the balsamy-
impulsive medicaments. The kiss-
sting of molasses consistency
(syrup-bitter hints iron not irony).

Thickened oil of a thousand counted lilies.
Oil of daffodil, oil of pheasant's eye.
Oil of must and oil of mayweed.
New myrrh and ling nut, the dregs of oil of saffron.
Knotted marjoram and oil of basil and oil of basil again.

"Pick me ..."

Pours it on thick as theriac the bush-
whacking physicians' treacly heal-alls.
The calls to arm thyself then the *Hail!*
Hail! pronouncements, the decrees.

The tinctures of vitriol, of Jesuit's bark.
The rough cathartics, the hell-
storming mercury. The bougies and fumes,
the fumigations, the fomentations.

Then equal parts bake-house and bagnio.
The poison-fed. The fever-starved. The
come-one-come-all the peccant-sweated.

*

Earth almond, cardamom.
True senna and mock sycamore.
Balm of Gilead, balm of Mecca.
New oil from unripe olives.
A half-pint purge of well-aged olive oil.

So Blooms the Aromatics
(those which warm the stomach, raise the pulse, quicken the circulation)

Rowan, Mountain Ash [Book 1.173]

Quickbeam guides the wayfarer.
Floral fossils and lamenting berries.
St. Valentine's under a rowan moon.
In woodland and grove. Near bog and burn.
Rows of fermenting fruit trees.

Charlatan ash. Quack ash.
Whitty pear and quicken-tree.
Trees of plastered waxwings.
Bohemian and sozzled on nostalgia.

mountain ash

Iris [Book 1.1]

Wild iris, flowering ring of grief and love lost.
With vinegar incises fatigue.
With honey cuts annoyance to the roots.

Bear Root, Bald-money [Book 1.3]

Glabrous bear root pounds the rheumatic chest.
Honeyed bald-money, kingly gentian.
Ruled by Mars in sunshine blue-starred and conspicuous.
Steep in wine to defeat stones and impediments.
Christen felwort for falls and sprains.
Draw a grassland hip bath for griping pain.

ninebark

Pomegranate, Carthaginian Apple [Book 1.151]

A wild pomegranate tree.
A tree that promises to explode.

Fruit as fragmenting bomb.
Fruit of the many-seeded dead.

Seeds of semiprecious provenance.
Seeds that detonate garnet.

Flowers that yield astringent dye.
Flowers that yield harsh nectar.

Nectar that keeps loose teeth fastened.
Nectar that stops the blood-spitter spitting.

A quick-witted pomologist gobs a spitball.
A fruitful pomologist lobs an apple-grenade.

Divine blood- and fire-filled.
Wind flowers and thunder claps.

Mercury offers up rain and tricks.
Mercury offers up subterfuge and flash.

Juniper [Book 1.103]

Whence the wind arises volatile juniper.
Unparalleled and solar.
The violent violet stench.
The serpent-driving fumes.

Burn the bark, scrape the dust from the wood.
Bitter berries expel bitter wind.
Oil of juniper remedies viper bite.
Spirit of juniper restores sore sight.

Sweet Flag, Sweet Sedge [Book 1.2]

Moon over bastard flag.
Summer gushes sweet rush and myrtle sedge.
Wild on the edge of pond and marsh.
Wild on the margins of lake and mud.

Where water overflows: Acorus.
Where moors overflow: False iris.
A retina of bees, the pupil of an eye.
The sidelong-glancing rhizome.

Cinnamon sedge, calamus and gladdon:
A spirituous tincture;
A recuperative cataplasm;
Passé poets and potestates;
A poultice by any other name.

A Caldarium of Bacteria

Through a halo of muscle-burn and fatigue.
Under swimming corpuscle light.
When the flora breaks down.
When the hedge is scraped naked.
So blooms the garden
of topical salves and microbial salvos.

Grime from the Baths   [Book 1.34]

Jupiter Vesuvius! this
Herculean accretion
of volcanic mineral
and metallic slag,
sheeps's tallow boiled
with cedar ash,
dust, skin, plaster—
scrapings from the bath.

Robust and rubicund
the rub a dub rubdown,
the salved, the weary,
the Attic-honeyed muscles
crushed. Rubbed ruddy,
rubbed raw—Gad!
God! the crud toe muck,
the goat soap scut.

Dubbed scrubwall.
Dubbed scrubland.

Grime from the Wrestling School [Book 1.35]

Uck the grimy volte-face mat reversal.
The hip heist. The headlock. The ankle pick.

Duck the high crotch leg setup (heralds
the wizzer, levels the lower body takedown).

Quick freestyle turn, back-flat, the mat rolls
a gazzoni, grunge-prone, RUB•A535-exposed.

Back-arch analgesic it, the tight waist, the cross-face,
the barrel roll-Voltaren, the lift, the switch, the sit out.

Grime from the Gymnasium Walls [Book 1.36]

Invigorating lengths of strength and beauty
(hamstrings, deltoids, squatted and planked)
amidst a calisthenics of mushroomy wall-covers.

The gym walls have cures. Spackling-salve,
putty-jam, plaster-dust dermabrasion. Tacky
gimcrackery to the training-naked ear.

The walls hung with fruit and wildlife,
flora and fond isometric reminiscence,
bird and anemone, poppy and peacock.

Near Running Water, Streams, and Creeks

The garden of living creatures.
The garden of honey and milk.
Of animal fat and frumentacea.
Of herbs endowed with spike and knife.
Of garlic and mustard and pungent kin.

Ass's liver while fasting.
Lungs of a fox for asthma.
Lungs of a swine for chafing and blisters.

Sea urchin for ulcers.
Hedgehog for convulsions.
Sea horse with goose grease for baldness.

Horse cheese. Horse's rennet.
Ewe's butter rubbed on ulcerated gums.
Whey for depression and elephantiasis.
Wormwood to feed Sardinian bees.

To assuage a headache: lanolin.
To accelerate scabs: burnt wool.
Beaver stones for wobbles, follicles and grease.
The belly of a weasel for venomous beasts.

So Blooms the Garden of Creatures of Land and Creatures of Sea

(products of dietetic and medicinal use)

backyard rabbit in April

Hare [Book 2.21]

Its brain for fear and trembling. Its curds to counter vertigo.

1

The land hare eats the hare's-foot fern for lunch.
A hare both herbaceous and herbivorous.
The rabbit's foot is a plant in prayer.
Low-lying, nocturnal.
A decumbent hare.

2

Apicius ranked entrées of hare second only to peacock.
An earth hare in earthenware.
A jugged hare.
A stewed in blood hare.
A hare pfeffered and braised.
A cat rousted from a roof and roasted as a hare.

3

The art of the hare is the art of not-showy blooms.
A drove of shrubby hares in well-drained soil.
A scroll of simple recipes.
First catch your hare.
Then RSVP the bees.

Sea Hare [Book 2.20]

As mad as a March hare under water.
Skittish floral reef and inky blooms.
Poof! A ruse of smoke and lose the wiry hair.

Sea hare crushed with sea nettles.
Sea hare cut with cuttlefish.
Sea hare a scuttling depilatory.

Orchis Hippopotamus [Book 2.25]

O stones of the river horse.
Dried and pounded and taken in wine.
Against viper bite and venom.
Against ill-intentioned intentions.
O the wide-mouthed floral displays.
The freshwater yawn spectacles.

Sheathfish [sic]   [Book 2.29]

A close cousin of Aristotle's catfish,
stoic sheathfish makes the voice sing.

A fish who sings adversity and enigma.
A fish who sings cooling pond and catastrophe.

"Freshwater or sarcophagus?" sings sheathfish.
"Eyeshine or particle emission?" sheathfish sings.

"Chuck the zone of alienation!
Who's the bottom-feeding top predator now?"

Sling mud at the mud cat, chuckle at the chucklehead,
charmed sheathfish makes the charged waters sing.

Lungs of the Sea   [Book 2.39]

Bioluminescent?
Gelatinous?
Sea plant or mollusc?
Sea grass or jellyfish?
Pulmo marinus
or *pneumon thalassios*?

Lungs lost at sea.
Lungs lost in misidentification.
Pound to small pieces and apply to chilblains.
Pound to small pieces and apply to gout.
(Strike that. Reverse it.)

Electric Ray [Book 2.17]

The lights are out and sores of long endurance lessen.

Lungs of a Fox [Book 2.41]

An earth breathing with lungs.
A lung skulk.
A lung leash.
Little fox lungs in the northern sky.
Lungs of yelp and combative call.
Lungs of growl and bark.

Fox lungs crushed, sifted and salted to taste.
Swift fox lungs for wheeze and cough.
Kit fox lungs for shortness of breath.

Cockroach [Book 2.38]

Carboniferous cockroach.
Gregarious cockroach.
Cockroaches who aggregate.
Cockroaches who shun the light.
Pound a millhouse cockroach with oil.
Boil a bakehouse cockroach to insect succulence.
Drip a drop in an ear to diminish an ache.
A dollop on the tongue to unlock the lungs.

Grasshopper [Book 2.56]

An aposematic poem.
Beginning of the End.[1]
Still life with grasshopper:
Flowers in a Vase (c. 1685);[2]
Flowers in a Vase with Shells and Insects (c. 1630).[3]
Take grasshoppers for the bladder roasted and bland.
Beware the warning coloration.
Beware the anti-predator adaptations.

---

[1] 1957 B movie in which giant grasshoppers attack Chicago.

[2] Painting by Rachel Ruysch.

[3] Painting by Balthasar van der Ast.

Earthworm [Book 2.72]

Dew-worm, rainworm, angleworm.
The annelidical worm who questions the soil.
The reciprocal worm who aerates the earth.
The skin-breathing worm (the gas-exchanger).
The mathematical worm who measures the depth.
The worm who cures both earache and toothache.
The worm who glues sinews torn apart.
Hence a small song for the multitasking worm.

Thus Some Cuttings of Book 3 and Book 4, the Virtues and the Roots, the Juices and the Herbs

(for uses both curative and quotidian)

Rhubarb [Book 3.2]

Great esculent garden.
Wisdom's sharp companion.
Patient rhubarb, wild rhubarb.
Beyond the Bosporus.
Beyond the pies lost
in a triangle of midsummer scruples.
Ginger and spikenard.
A dram of no misgivings.
A drop of caution under Mars.

Rue [Book 3.53]

A ring of rue around the neck.
A chaplet of rue.
Rue the tears of a weeping queen.
Fill a house with rue to kill the fleas.

Rue of contradiction and incongruity.
Rue vehement and full of grace.
Rue broody and distilled.
Rue impassioned and brewed.

Rue the rue that repeats itself—
once more the vinegar of the aforesaid four thieves.
The rue that dodged contagion.
The rue that robbed with impunity.

Sea Lavender [Book 4.16]

On the lake lip.
By the abdominal swamp.
In the subcosmopolis bog.

Limnal leaves in tufts.
Marsh rosemary.
Wild marsh beet of red seed.
Ink root.

For ancient ulcers.
For current events and topical discharge.
A drink of wine-dark limonium and sea.
A glass of sea thrift and wine.

Sparganium [Book 4.21]

At the edge of the water body.
Throat-choked and husky.
Rough-surfaced, *Burrr* ...
a lingual trill (bite your tongue!).

Reed-grass. Bur-reed. Branched
or simple-stem. With wine
ousts the venomous beast.
Brrr ... Cold-blooded,

the vocal chords a thick
vibrating trellis, rattling
snake fang and spiny
spherical lyrics. *That smarts!*-R's

renege the articulate,
breach the breath-contract.
With wine infuse both reed and root.
Compress and warm the wound.

Poppies Etc. [Book 4.64, 65, 66]

Superfluous poppies.

poppy pod back lane

Moon poppies and poppies under Leo.
Poppies of sea and poppies of field.
Poppies that blast the impassive.
Poppies that baste the wastrel to sleep.

Yellow-horned poppy flourishes in May.
A cordial corrective for ringworm and plague.
Wild poppy saturates May to July.
Douses holy fire, St. Anthony's fire,
hot ague and the burning urge to fall.

Scarlet countries of headache
(fields of corn rose and corn poppy).
Black poppy for tender eyes and offended ears.
White poppy procures rest and repose.
Sea poppy scatters ocular clouds.
Wild poppy lulls to lunar sleep.

Gladiolus [Book 4.20]

Staked straight the neck, the knife,
the wild iris forges forth. Little sword.
Unyielding sword lily. Blade-bolstered,
swaggering. Gladden the dagger leaves,
the steely rhizomes, with frankincense

and wine. A fume of few words.
A fetid anodyne. Stalks top-heavy,
woozy. The tipsy deadheads slip like fingers—
glazed and fused with honey-water and sun,
an opaque cornea flares a livid corona.

Prescribe a pale-sky corolla, an orange-red
burst of seed: as an antispasmodic; a cathartic;
a tweeze for prickles and stings. A decoction
of the lower root an effectual anaphrodisiac;
a decoction of the upper and the lust resumes.

elderberry

... and Lo Dearest Aerius,
In Unceasing Inquisitiveness. In Prudent Investigation.
With Gratitude. With Loving Benevolence. My Flowering Admiration.

APPENDIX A

NAMES OF PLANTS

Numerals refer to volume and entry in Dioscorides, Cul. to Culpeper,
Bot. to *Botanical.com*, Unk. to source unknown.

Planets, Stars, and Gods

Sunflower [Bot.]
Annual Mercury [4.191]
Dog's Mercury [4.192]
English Mercury [Bot.]
Mercury's Violet [4.18]
Three-seeded Mercury [4.94]
Venus's Hair [4.136]
Venus's Navelwort [4.92]
Earthgall [3.9]
Star of the Earth [2.158]
Jove's Beard [3.153]
Jupiter's Beard [4.89]
Moon Daisy [Bot.]
Moonstone [5.159]
Moon Trefoil [4.113]
Moonwort [3.105]
Star Anise [Bot.]
Starwort [2.214]
Autumnal-water Starwort [Cul.]
Garden Starwort [Cul.]
Sea Starwort [Cul.]
Star of Bethlehem [2.174; Bot.]
Great-Flowered Star of Bethlehem
    [2.201]
Yellow Star of Bethlehem [2.200]
Star of Hungary [Bot.]
Star Thistle [Cul.]
Hercule's Woundwort [Cul.]
Archangel [Cul.]

Blasphemes and Oaths

Adam's Apple! [1.166]
Bastard Agrimony! [4.59]
Bastard Hemp! [3.166]
Bastard Pellitory! [2.192]
Bastard Rocket! [2.170]

Bastard Rhubarb! [Cul.]
Bastard Sycamore! [1.181]
Bawd-Money! [4.124]
Bitter Vetch! [2.131]
Black Stinking Horehound! [3.117]
Blite and Wild Amaranth! [2.143]
Bush Vetch! [2.178]
By the Seed of the Lotus! [2.128]
Chaste Tree! [1.135]
Christ's Thorn! [1.121]
Cocculus! [4.48]
Darnel and Cheat! [2.116]
O Devil in a Bush! [1.46]
Devil's Spoons! [4.101]
Dry Rot! [1.112]
Fig! [1.183]
For the Love of Squirting Cucumbers!
    [1.54]
Fumitory! [4.110]
Good Laurel of Caesar! [4.147]
Great Monk's Rhubarb! [Cul.]
Gum Succory! [2.161]
Hoary Plantain! [2.153]
Holy Hemp! [4.95]
Holy Herb! [4.61]
Holy Wormwood! [3.28]
Homer's Moly! [3.54]
Livelong! [2.217]
Mare's Tail and Witches' Milk! [4.46]
Mother of Thousands Mind-your-own-
    business! [4.86]
Mother of Thyme! [3.44; Cul.]
Pig Nuts! [4.125]
Purging Buckthorn! [1.119]
Purging Croton! [4.164]
Scammony! [4.171]
Stinging Nettle! [4.94]
Stinking Motherwort! [4.49]

Stinkwort! [4.151]
Squill! [4.63]
Sweet Cicely! [4.116]
Sweet Maudlin! [4.59]
Sweet Virgin's Bower! [4.182]
Walnuts! [1.178]
Wild Bastard Cress! [2.186]
Wild Figs! [1.184]

Odds, Sods, and Improbabilities

Archangel [Cul.]
Ass of the Priest [3.47]
Brandy Bottle [3.149]
Candy Carrot [3.87]
Chihuahua Ash [Unk.]
Cinnamon Wattle [Unk.]
Common Enchanter's Nightshade [3.134]
Compass Plant [3.94]
Friars Cowl [2.198]
Langue de Bœuf [Cul.]
Military Orchid [3.141]
Pudding Grass [5.62]
Spring Snowflake [3.138]
Sticky Willy [3.104]
Turpentine Tree [5.39]

States of Mind and Manner

Bitter Apple [4.178]
Bitter Gourd [4.178]
Charity [4.8]
Chaste Tree [1.135]
Cheat [4.140]
Common Garden Patience [Cul.]
Flirtwort [Bot.]
Gold of Pleasure [4.117]
Great Garden Patience [Cul.]
Herb of Grace [3.52]
Herb True-love [Cul.]
Lily Constancy [Cul.]
Love in a Mist [3.93]
Madder [Cul.]
Madwort [Cul.]
Neglected Violet [4.122]
Petty Spurge [4.168; Cul.]
Poet's Cassia [4.143]

Prickly Samphire [Cul.]
Rue [3.52]
Sage of Virtue [Cul.]
Sassy Bark [Bot.]
Sea Wallflower [Cul.]
Sensitive Plant [Bot.]
Spunk [Cul.]
Sweet Maudlin [4.59]
Water Forget-Me-Not [4.195]
Wall Rue [4.15b]
Widow Wail [4.172]

Anatomy and Afflictions

Abscess Root [Bot.]
Acheweed [Bot.]
Adam's Apple [1.166]
All-Heal [Cul.; Bot.]
Arssmart [Cul.]
Arssmart, dead [Cul.]
Bindweed [Cul.]
Birthwort [Bot.]
Bladder Fucus [Bot.]
Bladder Herb [4.72]
Bladder Senna [Bot.]
Bladderwrack [4.100; Bot.]
Blister Plant [2.206]
Bloodwort [Cul.; Bot.]
Boneset [Bot.]
Consumptive's Weed [Bot.]
Cough-wort [Cul.]
Cramp Bark [Bot.]
Crown Marigold [4.58]
Eyebright [Cul.]
Feverberry [Bot.]
Feverfew [3.86; Bot.]
Feverfew, common [Cul.]
Feverfew, corn [Cul.]
Feverfew, sea [Cul.]
Feverfew, sweet [Cul.]
Feverwort [3.9]
Fingers, bloody [Bot.]
Fingers, lady's [3.153]
Fingers, dead man's [3.144]
Five Fingers Grass [4.42]
Gout-herb [Cul.]

Goutweed [Bot.]
Handflower [Bot.]
Hart's-horn [Cul.]
Hart's Tongue Fern [3.121; Bot.]
Hartwort [Cul.]
Headache [Cul.; Bot.]
Heartichoke [Cul.]
Heart Mint [Cul.]
Heart of the Earth [Bot.]
Heart's-ease [Cul.]
Heart Trefoil [Cul.]
Hepatica Triloba [Bot.]
Hurt-sickle [Cul.]
Kidney Beans [2.176]
Kidney-leaved Sowerweed [Cul.]
Kidney Vetch [3.153]
Kidneywort [Cul.; Bot.]
Knitbone [4.10]
Liver Balsam [4.29]
Liverleaf [Bot.]
Liverweed [Bot.]
Liverwort [4.41; Cul.; Bot.]
Liverwort, noble [Bot.]
(P)lumbago [5.100]
Lung Moss [Bot.]
Lungs, oak [Bot.]
Lungwort [4.150; Cul.; Bot.]
Memory Root [Bot.]
Nail-wort [Cul.]
Nailwort, thyme-leaved [4.54]
Navelwort [4.92]
Navelwort, sea [3.150]
Navelwort, Venus's [4.92]
Nipplewort [2.142; Cul.]
Nosebleed [4.103; Cul.]
Palsywort [Bot.]
Paralysis [Cul.]
Pilewort, common [Cul.]
Piss-a-bed [Cul.]
Prick Madam [Cul.]
Quinsy-wort [Bot.]
Rheum [Bot.]
Ribwort [Cul.; Bot.]
Ribwort, plantain [Cul.]
Rupture-wort [Cul.]
Sanguinaria [Cul.]

Sanguisorbia [Cul.]
Sciatica Cress [Cul.]
Sciatica Grass [Cul.]
Sciatica-wort [Cul.]
Scurvy Grass, common garden [Cul.]
Scurvy Grass, Dutch round-leaved [Cul.]
Scurvy Grass, horse-radish [Cul.]
Scurvy Grass, ivy-leaved [Cul.]
Scurvy Grass, sea [Cul.]
Self-heal [Cul.; Bot.]
Skeletonweed [Unk.]
Sneezewort [2.192; Cul.]
Sneezewort Yarrow [Cul.]
Spined Akantha, white [3.20]
Spleenwort, black [3.151]
Spleenwort, common [4.137; Cul.]
Swallow wort [2.211; Cul.]
Sweatroot [Bot.]
Tetterwort [Bot.]
Throat-wort [Cul.]
Tongue Grass [2.185]
Tongue, double [1.49]
Toothpick [3.60]
Toothwort [Cul.]
Umbilicus Veneris [Cul.]
Warty Spurge, annual [4.165g]
With-wind [Cul.]
Woundwort [3.120; Bot.]
Woundwort, clown's [Bot.]
Woundwort, hedge [4.35]
Woundwort, Hercule's [Cul.]
Woundwort, marsh [Bot.]
Woundwort, mountain [4.33]

Menagerie

Adder's Tongue [3.131; Cul.]
Bearberry [Bot.]
Bear Root [1.13]
Bear's Breeches [3.19; Cul.]
Bee Balm [3.118]
Bird's Eye [Bot.]
Bird's Foot [Cul.]
Bird's Foot Trefoil [4.112]
Bird Pepper [Cul.]
Buck's Horn [Cul.]

Buck's-horn Plantain [Cul.]
Bull's Foot [Cul.]
Bull Nettle [Bot.]
Bull-wort [Cul.]
Calf's Snout [4.133]
Calve's-foot [Cul.]
Calve's Snout [Cul.]
Camel Thorn [3.146]
Canary Grass [3.159]
Cat Mint [3.43; Cul.]
Cat's-foot [Cul.]
Cat's Milk [4.165d]
Cat's Tail [3.133]
Cat Thyme [3.124]
Caterpillar, common [4.195]
Chameleon, white [3.107]
Chickens, and hens [4.89]
Chickpea [2.126]
Chickweed [4.87]
Cock's Comb [Cul.]
Cock's Head [2.208; Cul.]
Cockspur [1.119]
Coltsfoot [3.126; Cul.]
Coltsfoot, sweet [4.108]
Cow Parsley [4.116]
Cow Parsnep [Cul.]
Cow Parsnip [4.67]
Cow Parsnip, common [3.55]
Cow Parsnip, downy [3.55]
Cow Parsnip, fig-leaved [3.55]
Cowslip [Cul.]
Cow Weed [4.116]
Crab's Claws [Cul.]
Crane's Bill [3.131; Cul.]
Crowfoot [2.206; Cul.]
Crowfoot Poppy [Cul.]
Cuckoo Flower [Cul.]
Cuckow Point [Cul.]
Deer's Tongue [Bot.]
Dog-berry [Cul.]
Dog Briar [1.123]
Dog Daisy [3.22]
Dog Fennel [Bot.]
Dog Rose [1.123; Cul.]
Dog's Arrach [Cul.]
Dog's-grass [Cul.]

Dog's Mercury [4.192; Cul.]
Dog's Mouth [4.143]
Dog's-tooth Violet [3.144]
Dog-teeth Violet [Cul.]
Dog Weed, mad [3.169]
Dogwood [1.172]
Dove's-foot [Cul.]
Dragon Arum [2.196a]
Dragonwort [2.196a]
Duck's-meat [Cul.]
Duckweed [4.88]
Duckweed, tropical [4.102]
Eagle Fern [4.187]
Fishbone Thistle [4.127]
Fleabane, great [3.136]
Flea Seed [4.70]
Flea-wort [Cul.]
Foal's-foot [Cul.]
Fox Geranium [3.131]
Foxglove [Bot.]
Fox Grape [4.183]
Frog's Foot [Cul.]
Gnat-like Orchid [3.144]
Goat Grass [4.139]
Goat's Arrach [Cul.]
Goat's Beard [2.173; Bot.]
Goat's Rue [Bot.]
Goat's Thorn [3.17]
Gooseberry [1.119; Cul.; Bot.]
Goosefoot [2.145; Bot.]
Goosefoot, purple [3.130]
Goosegrass [3.104]
Hare's Ear [Cul.]
Hare's Foot [4.17; Cul.]
Hawkbit [Bot.]
Hawkbit, autumnal [Bot.]
Hawkbit, mouse-ear [Bot.]
Hawkbit, rough [Bot.]
Hawkbit, wall [Bot.]
Hawkbit, wood [Bot.]
Hawkweed, wall [3.72]
Hawkweed, wood [3.72]
Hen-bane [Cul.]
Hen Bell [4.69]
Hen, fat [2.145; Bot.]
Hens, and chickens [4.89]

Hog Fennel [3.62; Cul.; Bot.]
Hogweed [3.90]
Horehound [Cul.]
Horehound, black stinking [3.117]
Horehound, foetid [3.117]
Horehound, white [3.38]
Horsebane [3.135]
Horse Chestnut [Bot.]
Horse Elder [1.27]
Horse Gowan [Bot.]
Horse-hoof [Cul.]
Horse Mint [3.42]
Horsenettle [Bot.]
Horse Parsley [1.78; Cul.]
Horse Radish [Cul.]
Horse-radish Scurvy Grass [Cul.]
Horse Sorrel [2.141]
Horsetail [Bot.]
Horsetail, barren [Bot.]
Horse Thyme [3.109]
Horse Tongue [4.147; Bot.]
Hound's Berry [4.74]
Hound's Tongue [4.129; Cul.]
Lamb's Tongue [Bot.]
Larkspur, tatra [3.84]
Lion's Foot [4.131]
Lion's Leaf [3.110]
Lion's Paw Cudweed [4.131]
Lion's Turnip [3.110]
Lizard Orchis [3.143]
Lousewort [4.156; Cul.]
Mare's Tail [4.46; Bot.]
Monkey Flower [Bot.]
Mouse Ear [2.214]
Mouse Ear, field [Cul.]
Mouse Ear Scorpion Grass [Cul.]
Mulewort [3.152]
Nymph, water [3.148]
Ox-eye Daisy [3.22; Bot.]
Ox-eye Daisy, yellow [3.156]
Oxlip [Cul.]
Ox-tongue [Bot.]

Oyster Plant [2.173]
Pelican Flower [Bot.]
Pheasant's Eye [4.161]
Pigeon's Grass [4.61]
Pig-nuts [Cul.]
Pigweed [Bot.]
Polecatweed [Bot.]
Robin, wake [Bot.]
Robin, golden wake [Cul.]
Robin, ragged [Cul.]
Scorpion Grass [Cul.]
Serpent's Tongue [Cul.]
Sheep Sorrel [Cul.; Bot.]
Sheep's Rampion [Cul.]
Skunk Cabbage [Bot.]
Sow Bread [2.194; Cul.]
Sow Fennel [Cul.]
Sowthistle [2.159]
Sow-thistle, common [Cul.]
Sowthistle, corn [3.72]
Sow-thistle, prickly [Cul.]
Sow-thistle, smooth [Cul.]
Sow-thistle Tree [Cul.]
Snake Bryony [4.184]
Snake Plant [2.196a]
Snakeroot [Bot.]
Snakeweed [Cul.; Bot.]
Sparrow Grass [2.152]
Spiderwort, lily [3.122]
Squirrel Corn [Bot.]
Swine-cress [Cul.]
Toadflax [4.133; Cul.; Bot.]
Turkey Corn [Bot.]
Turkey Pea [Bot.]
Wolf's Bane [4.77]
Wormseed, treacle [2.188]
Wormwood [3.26]
Wormwood, glacier [3.28]
Wormwood, holy [3.28]
Wormwood, sea [3.27]
Wormwood, silky [3.28]

APPENDIX B

Pedanius Dioscorides in His Backyard Plot, c. 2019

Once a riverbed. Now sediment and dead debris
like twigs, seeds, the birds dispersing gossip,
erroneous if well-meant. Fifty kilometers an hour
the wind plagues the neighborhood with desperation.
Jackhammer clouds, an outbreak of construction
—steely crashes, natter, rat-unrest. Hard at it
a hardhat surgical crew scrapes the myelin-piping
infrastructure. Exposed road grows pylon, famine weed.

In god's name the rototilling! The limb-sized roots.
A crypt of roots and endings. The digging never stops.
(When sun falls the medallion glass patio lanterns,
clementine and aquamarine, go up.) Clear-winged moths,
mosquitoes, a tease of tongue and ... not night-torpor,
more sardonic, scornful, then, like clockwork, a mockery
of egg-laying aphids (calling them plant lice calls up twice
the revulsion), dripping siphunculi, sticky honeydew, the piss.

APPENDIX C

GAZETTEER OF THE BACKYARD
(In Which Pedanius Dioscorides Takes Stock)

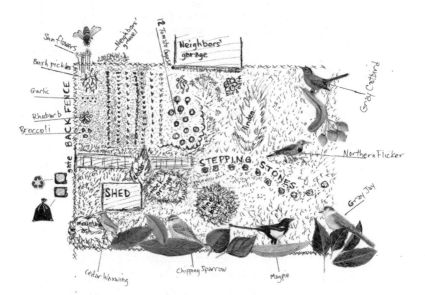

from aerial view of backyard

Part 1. Uprooted the Early Sky

1

Luminous flowers and luminous insects. Fire lilies and fireflies. *Heat confined on the Earth by the Air.* Evening star in the low west. Northern flickers, starlings, phosphorus and August.

Perseids seed the 3b hardiness zone. A zone of zahara starlight zinnias. Double clusters and heliotropes, sunflowers under Swift-Tuttle showers. Orbits of high-heaped cloudberries. A royal poet of a sky!

2

Morning cock-crows an aurora of Phoenician purple and Tyrian sea-snail. By last night's leaf the embroidery ladies talked and walked me off my legs! "The garden is a three-fold mahogany screen with hollyhock and sweet-pea. A weave of violet and bindweed with a weft of aristocratic toga." O thorn and thistle me already.

3

How many bags of sheep shit? How many bales of peat? Ten weeks of drought, eight weeks of deluge and gloom. The odd sunny day with a wind that knocks the bean stalks flat on their backs. And the weeds ...

My rows bode bad with wode whistle, cheatgrass, bad man's oatmeal, and yolky toad-flax—a blunder garden! The missteps, the false alyssum, the prolifically prolix knapweed ... a pervasive invasive creep. Taproots tapping my optimism.

4

A yard is not a yard without birds. The front beds dense with crowfoot violet, bloody cranesbill. The lawn a skirmish of gooseneck loosestrife and chickweed. Back here *by Jupiter's beard* the magpies plunder my seed heads, a sharp-shinned hawk skewers the view from the neighbor's garage. Gayfeather, the sparrows, Veronica, the wandering chickadees, blue spikes and jays, flecked plumage.

On the south side of the yard, rowan berries, Siberian peashrub, ninebark slough. The fipple-winded linden (that heart-leaved stalwart) is the backyard axis mundi. *Mother of thousands thrice* the brindled catbird's mewed! Gray catbird sings from the catbird seat, a high-branch fermata, a basswood basso continuo, a sustained hush-hush surveillance.

5

Ten degrees and counting to the waggle-forage, the waggle-run, the long-corolla bee balm, the catmint, the nasturtium. Magnanimous bees and magnanimous bee plants. Holy hyssop purges the soil, woos the gypsy cuckoo bumblebee. *Bombus borealis* whoops the virtues of Venus, the whorled mint, the wild horsemint, the mint of no remorse.

Honeyberry, sweetberry, blue-berried honeysuckle. Waxy haskap buffs bee dreams and bullseye vision, a dance of flicker-victory and bee's purple. Behold primrose and pansy, spectrum-nectared rudbeckia, heliopsis summer sun.

6

Bamboozled as a confusing bumblebee. My bull-thistled fingers, my wilting boxelder back—I've become an ornamental crab! All this number-crunching and cruciferae. *Sweet maudlin* what a cross to bear this humble garden has! Onion-eyed I cry just to look at that back fence ... Answer me, dead broccoli! A tragic trio bolts a crop of bad hair and halitosis.

True to nature the ungainly crushes the tightfisted: the rhubarb overgrown, the garlic (after two years) unforthcoming. At the far end of the fence a pint-sized bush of pint-sized pickles, then rows of bleeding beets, vulgar red-cheeked chard, and the peas, the peas, the peas (rattling all night in their pods, my dreams are noisy with the poison of peas).

Bastard rhubarb ... the mock orange at the northeast corner of the shed lampoons me with pruning ridicule. Have I been as caustic as petty spurge, madwort and madder yet? Not as I thought a sage of virtue but an oversensitive sensitive plant?

Notwithstanding my chipped and crumbling birdbath (spurned by finch and siskin alike), a mere northwest step from the stepping stones are twelve prolific tomato cages (big beef hybrid, bodacious hybrid, bumblebee mix), copious constellations of carrots (lunar white and solar yellow), and the flowers ... moonflower, moon violet, star grass, shooting star and star-flowered lily of the valley. *Sweet virgin's bower* a virtual galaxy of a garden!

Part 2. A Perennial Saga (Before the Blue Lake Bush Beans, the Bolero Hybrid Carrots, the Maestro Peas, the Ruby Queen Beets)

1

Gardens over long-gone lakes. Over fluvial plains. Over lacustrine plains. Aeolian or wind-worked. Over pitted outwash plains. Over mixed knoll and depression.

Gardens of orthic dark brown soil. Calcareous dark brown. Eluviated dark brown. Humic gleysols.

Soils moderately fine to fine-textured. Moderately calcareous usually saline. Clayey glacio-lacustrine deposits. Unsorted glacial till.

Gardens of nearly level topography. Of topography gently sloping or roughly undulating. Moderately sloping or gently rolling. Strongly sloping or moderately rolling. Steeply sloping or strongly rolling.

2

Gardens with perennials that mimic black coral branching like a tree. That mimic saffron-colored laminated rocks. With rows that mimic sea froth, salt flowers, a river with a crust of bicolored daylily.

Gardens with the temperament of pumice stone that stops boiling wine boiling. Of alkaline earth that restrains the tongue. With the constitution of whetstone that mollifies major and minor organs. With the antiseptic nature of adamantine spar.

Gardens of unambiguous moss. Opportunistic moss. Outbreaks of rockbreak, bear's bed, robin's eye. Gardens of anonymous moss and closeted moss (Iceland moss a lichen that passes as a moss). Moss that conquers lassitude. Moss that comforts the heart.

The gardens of unwanted plants and persistence. Lamb's-quarters, shepherd's purse, purslane. The argumentative and self-important gardens. Prostrate knotweed, supercilious stinkweed, black medic.

Part 3. Asclepiads

What I wish you could see in this crudely rendered drawing...

A metrical line from plant to poet to the god of physicians. A geology of medicine and herb. Not companion planting but conviviality. Plants doting on stones, metals smitten with flowers.

Asclepios cut open the earth, restored the heart's beat to the dead. Milkweed took the garden's pulse, deemed it butterfly- and bee-fluent.

A diagnosis was made, of dactyls like waterweed, of rose-stanza silkweed, of a lyre heart-strung and serpent-wound.

zahara starlight zinnia

APPENDIX D

MAP OF MEDICAL MATERIALS

province of Saskatchewan with Dioscorides

APPENDIX D (1)

Legend

1. Aromatics
Mixed grass, flowers, oil, and sap. Corn-rose under rising moon. Meadow saffron under Saturn. Poppy resin and a blood-firing ecotone. Where blooms blossom algae, where scarcely a wheeze breezes sea rush into lungs of the sea.

2. Living Creatures
Aspen groves and grassland. Amidst beaked willow and red osier dogwood a medicinal of the winged and the furred, the shelled and the finned. Mesic-wet and mixedwood, where hare meets rabbitfoot-grass, where rattlesnake plantain sloughs the skin of a yellowbelly racer.

3. Roots
Cool summers and cold winters. Naked in plain sight the hidden lines of rock-brake fern, parsley fern, dense cryptic fronds. Dig down and crack the curative cypher. The forest buttressed by a pharmacopeia of roots and … holdfast! The gall, the earthgall! O horehound, O mother of thyme!

4. Other Herbs and Roots; Narcotic Plants
Woodlands and shrubland borders. *Darnel, and all the idle weeds that grow*. Bur reed and wild rye. Governed by the moon the perfection of dog-tooth, the smooth brome, the nodding-off brome. Till the leaf falls the sweet sleep-inducing vernal grass.

5. Earth and Metallic Stones
Let this suffice: the story under the understory. The story under tamarack and trembling aspen, under jack pine and black spruce. Under bog and calypso orchid, under heart-leaved twayblade. Earth, earth and stone, sand heated by sun. Clay, palladium, silica, zinc. Fossilized oyster shell, pine cones turned to stone, earth to wither tumors, earth to poultice a wound.

APPENDIX E

Topography of Repeating Plants and Patterns

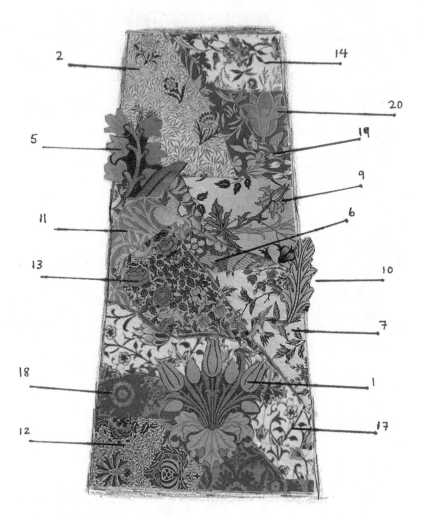

province of Saskatchewan with William Morris

APPENDIX E (1)

Legend

1. Tulips among a grass of worsted warp.
2. Leaves peppered with carnations and peonies.

3. Honeysuckle and myrtle (one entwines linen, one adorns a wall).
4. Sunflower and acanthus leaves in a garden of combed cotton and silk.

5. Block-printed bluebells on cotton and linen.
6. A simple appliqué design of pomegranates and foliage.

7. Elegantly worked trees with hopelessly stylized birds.
8. Branches of hummingbird and crested bird on printed cotton.

9. Honeysuckle and briar on cream-colored ground.
10. A design of curving leaves.

11. Vine and pomegranates on 3-ply carpeting.
12. Pomegranates and foliage in pink and green silk.

13. Rosebush and apple tree cushion covers.
14. Morning glory and bindweed cushion covers.

15. Artichokes and thistles in gold thread and silk.
16. A 4-part mohair colorway of violet and columbine.

17. Daffodil-, willow bough-, and rambling rose-printed cotton.
18. Acorn embossed on silk velvet.

19. Medieval designs with sunflowers and daisies.
20. Dyes as old as Pliny: chestnut, plum, saffron, madder.

3

4

8

15

16

Persian shield

Let this suffice ...

Notes and Sources

"The Garden Body": Number 6 incorporates some lines from and references to Erasmus Darwin's "The Botanic Garden." In number 7, "Red as any rose" is from Shakespeare's *Henry IV*, Part 2. In number 10, the viola organista was a musical instrument designed (but never constructed) by Leonardo da Vinci. The writings of Nicholas Culpeper echo throughout this sequence, however his work has had an inestimable influence on all of *Garden Physic*.

"*Equisetum hyemale* (Rough Horsetail)": The photograph that this poem responds to can be found in *Karl Blossfeldt, The Alphabet of Plants* (Munich: Schirmer Art Books, 2007).

"Grasscloth (Millefleur)": *Scroll*, *Littlescroll*, *Flora*, *Sistine*, and *Trinitas* are names of William Morris patterns.

"Wallpaper": *Poppy* and *Wreath* are names of William Morris patterns.

"William Morris in His Disappointment Garden": *Little Chintz* and *Corncockle* are names of William Morris patterns.

"Floral Correspondences": In "My Darling," the first poem of this series, "Suns sink on suns" is from Erasmus Darwin's "The Botanic Garden."

"Pedanius Dioscorides in His Backyard Plot": "crypt of roots and endings" is from number IV of Geoffrey Hill's *Mercian Hymns* (London: André Deutsch, 1971).

"Gazetteer of the Backyard": In Part 1.1, "Heat confined on the Earth by the Air" is from Erasmus Darwin's "The Botanic Garden." In Part 1.4, "thrice the brindled catbird's mewed" is a variation on a line from *Macbeth*.

"Appendix D (1)": In entry number 4 of the Legend, "Darnel, and all the idle weeds that grow" is from *King Lear*.

...

Numerous works were essential to the writing of *Garden Physic*, most notably:

Pedanius Dioscorides (c. 40–90 AD), *de Materia Medica*. Various versions of this work can be found online (e.g., Google Books and World Digital Library).

Nicholas Culpeper (1616–1654), *The Complete Herbal* (London: Imperial Chemicals (Pharmaceuticals), 1953).

Many randomly encountered field guides and books on botany and horticulture were consulted—too many to mention. However, I am particularly indebted to the six fascicles of *Flora of Saskatchewan*, published jointly by Flora of Saskatchewan Association and Nature Saskatchewan (2011–2018). "Ferns and Fern Allies" and "Catkin-Bearing Trees and Shrubs" take their names from the titles of Fascicle 1 and Fascicle 5 respectively.

William T. Stearn's *Botanical Latin* (4th Edition. Portland: Timber Press, 2004) was an invaluable resource, as was *Botanical.com*.

Erasmus Darwin's (1731–1802) "The Botanic Garden" (which includes "The Loves of the Plants" and "The Economy of Vegetation") served as a model of theatrically rococo language. Originally published in 1791, this work is available as an eBook through Project Gutenberg.

For textiles and patterns of William Morris (1834–1896) I often consulted Linda Parry, *William Morris Textiles* (London: V&A Publishing, 2013).

The paintings of Agnes Martin (1912–2004), who was originally from Macklin, Saskatchewan, have been floating in the back of my head for many years but finally bubbled into this collection after I saw a retrospective of her work at the Guggenheim in 2016.

Allusions to Vita Sackville-West's (1892–1962) "moon garden" aka "white garden" entered my poetry approximately twenty years ago when I wrote a long poem titled "Negative Garden." Though "Floral Correspondences" is an entirely invented exchange, the following works were instrumental to my thinking about and composition of this sequence:

Vita and Harold: The Letters of Vita Sackville-West and Harold Nicolson, edited by Nigel Nicolson (New York: G.P. Putnam's Sons, 1992).

The Letters of Vita Sackville-West to Virgina Woolf, edited by Louise DeSalvo and Mitchell A. Leaska (London: Hutchinson & Co., 1984).

And the following, by Vita Sackville-West: *The Illustrated Garden Book* (New York: Antheneum, 1986) and *Some Flowers* (London: National Trust Books, 2014), as well as her poetry collection *The Garden* (London: Michael Joseph Limited, 1946).

Index

Titles in italics, first lines of untitled poems in roman type.

Acknowledgments

Thank you to the editors of the following publications and venues where some of these poems have previously appeared.

"Cockroach," "Ferns and Fern Allies," "Origins of the Poem," and "Prelude" were first published by *Granta Online* (January 2021).

"Corn Crowfoot, Corn Buttercup" was first published in *The New York Review of Books* (April 9, 2020).

"Gazetteer of the Backyard" was first published in *Poetry* (March 2020).

Six poems from "Floral Correspondences" were first published in *The Paris Review* (Winter 2019).

"Rhubarb," "Rue," and "Sea Lavender" were audio-recorded as part of the Faber & Faber Poetry Podcast #10 (Fall 2019), hosted by Rachael Allen and Jack Underwood.

"Flowers of Brass" and five poems from "Floral Correspondences" were first published in *Music & Literature: No. 9* (April 2019).

"Habitat" and "Near Running Water, Streams, and Creeks" were first published in *New American Writing* 37 (2019).

"The Garden Body: A Florilegium" was first published in *Poetry* (October 2018).

"White Flower II" was first published in *Border Crossings* (September 2018).

"Plants Reduced to the Idea of Plants" and "Plants Further Reduced to the Idea of Plants" were first published (with different titles) in *Kenyon Review* (May/June 2018).

"Sparganium" was first published as a broadside by *Arc Poetry Magazine* (2018).

"Grasscloth 1," "Grasscloth (Millefleur)," and (with different titles) "So Blooms (the remedial florilegia)," "So Blooms (a vial of *viola tricolor*)," "'Struth," and "Pick Me (Peals the self-serving physic garden)" were first published by *Granta Online* (November 2017).

"Viola," "Violet," and "Root of Scarcity" were first published in *Poetry* (October 2017).

"William Morris in His Disappointment Garden" and "Pedanius Dioscorides in His Backyard Plot" were first published in *Conjunctions Online* (February 2017).

"Pick Me (Pours it on thick …)" and "The Dedication" were first published in *New American Writing* 34 (Summer 2016).

...

I am exceedingly grateful to the Canada Council for the Arts and to the Saskatchewan Arts Board for funding that bought me time to work on *Garden Physic*.

For their support and encouragement special thanks go out to Rachael Allen, Susan Andrews Grace, Taylor Davis-Van Atta, Paul Hoover, Barbara Langhorst, Daniel Peña, and Don Share. Thanks to Van Broste for his horticultural expertise and for letting me steal leaves from his garden.

My heartfelt appreciation to everyone at New Directions, especially Jeffrey Yang, Barbara Epler, Brittany Dennison, Mieke Chew, Declan Spring, and Erik Rieselbach. Thanks as well to Erik Carter for the cover design that I loved on first sight, and to Marian Bantjes for the exquisite interior design.

Most importantly, my deep love and gratitude to Guy Vanderhaeghe, to whom this collection is dedicated, who wholeheartedly encouraged me to turn the backyard into a living, messy, rabbit-teeming experiment.